Word JAM

n. 1. An ELECTRIFYING, MESMERIZING, GRAVITY-DEFYING Guide to a POWERFUL and AWESOME Vocabulary

Walt "Clyde" Frazier

NBA Hall of Famer and TV Broadcaster

illustrated by Donna Reynolds

D0187782

Thanks to Joanne Mattern.

Special thanks to Avonelle Pole for providing the impetus and enlightenment to the omnipotence of words!

Art direction by Pisaza Design Studio, Ltd.

Word
JAM

Word JAM

How I Started Loving Words

I was a superb basketball player in my day. When I was playing with the New York Knicks, they won the only two championships in that team's history. I was proud to be a part of those teams. When I played pro basketball, I had a reputation for being cool. Some people said I didn't even sweat when I was on the court! I personified this image off the court as well.

When I retired from my playing career, it was still important for me to be myself and enjoy what I was doing. Today I do that through the magic of words. Now I'd like to pass some of that magic along to you.

In 1989, I started doing pre-game shows and halftime shows for the Knicks. At first I broadcast on the radio, and later I appeared on TV. I quickly discovered that I'd better know what I was talking about—and be articulate. When I started out in broadcasting, I had only two minutes to speak my piece. Two minutes is not a long time. If I didn't know what I wanted to say, I would end up being redundant and incoherent. That's not my concept of professionalism.

I figured the more words I knew, the more confident and effective I would be. So I started learning about words. Wherever I went, I carried books with me. Pocket dictionaries and wordbooks were my best friends. I also made lists: lists of power words that made my speech provocative and created vivid images, lists of words that alliterated and devastated.

Along the way, I've discovered that words are like people. Each word conveys a different meaning and has a different personality. Some words make you feel bad, while others lift you up. The more words you know, the more you can sparkle and show your stuff.

Now that's what I call cool.

Walt "Clyde" Frazier

How to Use This Book

I wrote this book because I wanted to help you learn new words and how to use them. Each chapter starts with a story that uses ten to twelve power words—words that jump out and grab you with their rhythm and reason. After you read the story and see how the words are utilized, take a closer look at the words themselves. For each power word, I've clued you in on how to pronounce it, what part of speech it is, and what it means.

But I didn't stop there! Each power word has an etymology, or story behind it. Check out my "Fast-Break Facts" for a quick look at the word's history—what language it comes from, what it used to mean, how long it's been part of our English vocabulary, and other forms of the word. Finally, I've included a list of synonyms—words that mean the same thing. Think of these as bonus words to give you an even more powerful vocabulary!

Once you've gone through the book, it's time to make these words your own. Remember, if you don't use them, you lose them. Just like hanging with new friends, the more time you spend with these words, the more you'll understand them and feel comfortable with them. You'll be surprised at how wonderful these words will make you feel. And that's the kind of joy that can help you achieve your dreams!

1

Aliens Among Us?

Zak is a space alien disguised as an ordinary student. He was sent to Earth to observe our behavior. Here's his latest report back to his commanding officer.

Report to the Commander

To: Space Commander Zorgon
From: Zak
Re: Earthling Behavior

Dear **Esteemed** Commander:

Today I observed Earthling teenagers at a school dance. It was a most unusual experience.

The dance was held in the school gym. When I entered, the noise was **cacophonous**. A **multitude** of boys and girls were dancing to music that pulsated through the air. The music was so loud that the Earthlings had to **screech** to be heard above the **uproar**.

Watching the Earthlings dance **fascinated** me. They threw their bodies back and forth with abandon. The Earthlings didn't seem to care when they **jostled** one another. Walking across the crowded dance floor was like making my way through a dangerous **labyrinth**.

On one side of the gym was a table. A crowd of Earthlings stood before it to **procure** food and drink. There were many **delectable** offerings, including crunchy, thin wafers called potato chips and a fizzy liquid called soda. I must confess, I was not **timid** about consuming large quantities of these tasty foods.

In closing, I **contend** that the Earthlings' behavior was quite bizarre. But they seemed to be enthralled by this social event.

Since Zak learned English by memorizing a dictionary, he used lots of big words in his report. Take a look at some of the power words in his word jam.

....

cacophonous (kuh-KAH-fuh-nuss) (*adjective*)—an incredibly noisy jumble of unpleasant sounds.

The out-of-tune orchestra made a **cacophonous** noise as it warmed up.

 FAST-BREAK FACTS:

- The *noun* form of this word is **cacophony**.
- **Cacophonous** comes from a Greek word, *kakophonos*. In Greek, *phonos* means "voice" or "sound."

 YOU COULD ALSO SAY:
discordant, dissonant, harsh

....

contend (kuhn-TEND) (*verb*)—to make a point in a discussion.

I **contend** that you were wrong to eat all the chocolate brownies.

 FAST-BREAK FACTS:

- The *adjective* **contentious** comes from the word **contend**.
  A **contentious** person is always ready to disagree with you.
- **Contend** can also mean to compete with someone.
  That's where we get the *noun* **contender**.
- **Contend** comes from an old French word, *contendre*.
  Contendre means "to stretch."

 YOU COULD ALSO SAY:
argue, assert, insist

---

delectable (dih-LEK-tuh-buhl) (*adjective*)—highly pleasing.
Usually used to describe really delicious food.

The strawberries from Mom's garden were **delectable** with whipped cream.

 FAST-BREAK FACTS:

- The *noun* form of this word is **delectability**.
  The *adverb* is **delectably**.
- **Delectable** comes from the Latin word *delectare*, which means "to delight."

 YOU COULD ALSO SAY:
delicious, pleasing, satisfying, luscious

esteem (iss-TEEM) (*noun*)—respect or admiration.

Kelly held her soccer coach in high **esteem**.

 ## FAST-BREAK FACTS:

- **Esteem** can also be used as a *verb*.
- **Esteem** comes from the Latin word *aestimare*. We get the word estimate from *aestimare* too. To **estimate** something is to judge its value. **Esteem** means to value something highly. See the connection?

 ## YOU COULD ALSO SAY:
awe, honor, admiration, regard

---

fascinate (FAH-suhn-ate) (*verb*)—to hold your attention in a big way.

The sound of the music box **fascinated** the baby.

 ## FAST-BREAK FACTS:

- The *noun* form of this word is **fascination**.
- This word has an unusual background. It's from the Latin *fascinum*, which means "an evil spell." One early meaning of **fascinate** was "to bewitch." But the word's meaning has changed over the years, and it no longer has anything to do with witches or spells!

 ## YOU COULD ALSO SAY:
captivate, charm, enthrall, enchant

jostle (JAH-suhl) (*verb*)—to bump or push roughly.

The referee called a foul when Cal **jostled** a player on the other team.

FAST-BREAK FACTS:

- This word is an alteration of an old English word, *justle*, which was another way of saying **joust**. A **joust** was a sport in which a knight rode toward another knight and tried to knock him off his horse—or **jostle** him to the ground!

YOU COULD ALSO SAY:
jar, shove, upset, nudge

labyrinth (LAH-buh-rinth) (*noun*)—something that is confusing or complicated to get through.

I got lost walking through the **labyrinth** of city streets.

FAST-BREAK FACTS:

- This word comes from the Greek *labyrinthos*. In Greek myth, a man named Daedalus built an incredible maze, called the **Labyrinth**, for King Minos. A horrible monster called the Minotaur guarded the **Labyrinth**.
- For a really big word, try saying **labyrinthine**. That's the *adjective* form of **labyrinth**. It means "intricate" or "involved."

YOU COULD ALSO SAY:

maze, complex, puzzle

---

multitude (MUHL-tuh-tood) (*noun*)—a huge number of people or things.

There was a **multitude** of people at the sold-out game.

FAST-BREAK FACTS:

- The *adjective* form of this word is **multitudinous**.
- The word **multitude** comes from several old English, French, and Latin words. But the root of all of them is the Latin *multos*, which means "many."

YOU COULD ALSO SAY:

myriad, profusion, abundance

---

procure (proh-KYUR) (*verb*)—to get your hands on.

Brandon will **procure** the food for tonight's party.

FAST-BREAK FACTS:

- The word **procure** is from two Latin words: *pro*, which means "for," and *cura*, which means "care."
- Someone who **procures** is called a **procurer**. And **procuring** something can be called **procurement**. Both of those words are *nouns*.

YOU COULD ALSO SAY:
acquire, gain

....

screech (SKREECH) (*verb*)—to make a high, harsh, unpleasant sound.

Nedra **screeched** when her brother poured ice down her shirt.

FAST-BREAK FACTS:

- **Screech** can also be used as a *noun*. A **screech** is the sound made when you . . . well . . . **screech**!
- **Screech** is an example of onomatopoeia. That's a fancy term for using a word that sounds like the thing it stands for. *Buzz, bang,* and *sizzle* are other examples of onomatopoeia.
- The word **screech** has been around since 1560! It's an alteration of an earlier English word, *scritch*. That word may have come from an Old Norse word, *skraekja*.
- There is a bird called the **screech** owl. You can imagine what it sounds like!

YOU COULD ALSO SAY:
scream, shriek

....

timid (TIH-mid) (*adjective*)—shy and fearful.

The new student was too **timid** to tell us his name.

FAST-BREAK FACTS:

- The *noun* form of this word is **timidity**. And if you do something in a **timid** way, you do it **timidly**. That word is an *adverb*.
- **Timid** is another word that comes from Latin. This time, the Latin word is *timere*, which means "to fear."

YOU COULD ALSO SAY:
apprehensive, cowardly, fainthearted, bashful

---

uproar (UHP-rohr) (*noun*)—a lot of shouting and noise.

When our team won the championship, the game ended in an **uproar**.

FAST-BREAK FACTS:

- The *adjective* form of this word is **uproarious**. Along with meaning "noisy," **uproarious** can also mean "very funny."
- This word comes from two different sources. There is an old Dutch word, *oproer*, which means "up" and "motion." There's also a similar word in Old English. That word is *hreran*, which means "to stir."

YOU COULD ALSO SAY:
chaos, commotion, disorder, tumult

2

A Letter to the Editor

Lisa was livid when the local newspaper failed to report her school's basketball games. So she wrote this letter to the editor of the newspaper.

Dear Editor,

Your **apathetic** attitude concerning Ridge High School's basketball team **baffles** me. What could be your reasons for not including our school in your sports reports?

It's true that Ridge High is a small school with a **fledgling** team that only started playing last year. But our school is not so **minuscule** that you can completely ignore us! After all, **throngs** of people come to all our games!

Although our team consists of **novices**, it is not made up of **immature** players. In fact, just the opposite is true. The captain was **nominated** for Player of the Year last season. And everyone plays with great **zeal** and dedication.

Our students and their families read your newspaper and pay attention to your words. We are **irate** that you don't pay attention to us!

I don't mean to **berate** or **criticize** you, but I hope you will change your mind and report on Ridge High's games in the future.

Sincerely,

Lisa Smith

Because Lisa was so mad when she wrote this letter, she filled her word jam with some real power words! Let's take a look at what they mean.

---

apathetic (ah-puh-THEH-tik) (*adjective*)—Who cares? No, really, this word describes someone who couldn't care less.

Our team was so bad, I felt **apathetic** about playing.

FAST-BREAK FACTS:

- The *noun* form of this word is **apathy**.
- The word **apathetic** comes from a Greek word, *apathes*, which means "without feeling."

YOU COULD ALSO SAY:
indifferent, dispassionate, listless

---

baffle (BAH-fuhl) (*verb*)—to confuse.

The math problem **baffled** John.

FAST-BREAK FACTS:

- If something **baffles** you, then you could say it was **baffling**. **Baffling** is an *adjective*.
- **Baffle** comes from an old Scottish word, *bawchillen*, which means to say something bad about someone in public.

YOU COULD ALSO SAY:
befuddle, puzzle, fluster, perplex

---

berate (bih-RATE) (*verb*)—to really lay into someone, to scold him or her loudly for a long time.

When I didn't do my homework, Mom **berated** me for what seemed like hours.

FAST-BREAK FACTS:

• The word **berate** has been around since 1548!

YOU COULD ALSO SAY:
castigate, chide, rebuke, scold

---

criticize (KRIH-tuh-size) (*verb*)—to tell someone what he or she has done wrong.

Coach **criticized** Ned for missing all his foul shots.

FAST-BREAK FACTS:

• The *noun* form of this word is **criticism**.
• If you spend a lot of time **criticizing,** you might be described by the *adjective* **critical**. Or you might be called a **critic**, which is a *noun*.
• The word **criticize** has been around since 1649 and comes from a Greek word, *kritikos*, which means "to discern" or "to judge."

YOU COULD ALSO SAY:
disparage, reproach, condemn

Fledgling

fledgling (FLEJ-ling) (*noun*)—an inexperienced person.

The rookies were just **fledglings**, so they didn't play in many games.

 FAST-BREAK FACTS:

- A **fledgling** is also the name of a baby bird before it has its feathers and learns how to fly. See the connection?
- **Fledgling** is a pretty new word—it has only been around since 1830.

 YOU COULD ALSO SAY:
neophyte, novice

---

immature (ih-muh-CHUR) (*adjective*)—behaving in a childish manner.

Nicole acts so **immature**, it's embarrassing to be around her.

 FAST-BREAK FACTS:

- **Immature** comes from the Latin word *immaturus*. In Latin, *im* means "not," and *maturus* means "mature."
- The *noun* form of this word is **immaturity**.

 YOU COULD ALSO SAY:
infantile, juvenile, puerile

irate (eye-RATE) (*adjective*)—really, really angry.

Dad was **irate** when my sister came home late.

 ## FAST-BREAK FACTS:

- **Irate** comes from the word **ire**. **Ire** is a *noun*, and it's another word for "anger."
- This word comes from the Latin word *iratus*, which means "to be angry."

 ### YOU COULD ALSO SAY:
furious, incensed, indignant, choleric

....

minuscule (MIH-nuhs-kyool) (*adjective*)—incredibly tiny.

Germs are so **minuscule**, you can't see them without a microscope.

 ## FAST-BREAK FACTS:

- **Minuscule** comes from the Latin word *minusculus*, which means "small."
- A word that sounds a lot like **minuscule** and means the same thing is **minute** (pronounced my-NOOT).

 ### YOU COULD ALSO SAY:
infinitesimal, tiny, insignificant, lilliputian

....

nominate (NAH-muh-nate) (*verb*)—to suggest someone for a job or for an award.

Wayne's coach **nominated** him for Rookie of the Year.

 ## FAST-BREAK FACTS:

- This word comes from the Latin *nominare*, which means "to name."
- Someone who is **nominated** is called a **nominee**. That word is a *noun*.

 ## YOU COULD ALSO SAY:
choose, designate, suggest, propose

---

novice (NAH-vuhs) (*noun*)—a beginner.

Even though Lynn is a **novice**, she is one of the best players on the team.

 ## FAST-BREAK FACTS:

- **Novice** comes from the Latin word *novus*, which means "new."

 ## YOU COULD ALSO SAY:
apprentice, amateur, beginner, neophyte

throng (THRONG) (*noun*)—a large crowd of people.

Hannah pushed through the **throng** to get to the front of the line.

 ## FAST-BREAK FACTS:

- **Throng** can also be used as a *verb*. To **throng** means to crowd together.
- This word is from the old English *thringan,* which means "to press" or "to crowd."

 ## YOU COULD ALSO SAY:
crowd, host, multitude

zeal (ZEEL) (*noun*)—great eagerness or interest.

To please her parents, Mona cleaned her room with **zeal**.

 FAST-BREAK FACTS:

- Someone who has a lot of **zeal** is known as a **zealot**. That word is a *noun*. If you do something with a lot of **zeal**, you could be described as **zealous**—an *adjective*.
- **Zeal** comes from a Greek word, *zelos*.

 YOU COULD ALSO SAY:
enthusiasm, fervor, zest

RaBid

In My Opinion

3

Kevin writes movie reviews for an on-line magazine. Here's his review of the latest action flick.

Destiny Masters Misses the Mark

Throw in enough car chases, violent explosions, and fight scenes, and you'll have a successful movie, right? Wrong! The new film *Destiny Masters* does just that, and it is nothing better than **mediocre**.

The main problem with this movie is the characters. They are all as flat as a piece of cardboard. You can tell who the hero is because of his **rugged** good looks. He also **swaggers** through every scene. The hero has a **loquacious** girlfriend. Of course, her perpetual chatter gets everyone in trouble. Then there is the bad guy. He has a **rabid** look in his eyes and a **sullen** attitude. You know he's up to no good as soon as he steps on-screen!

The plot is **cumbersome** too. It has something to do with a **scheme** to **ambush** the president of the United States, but the action happens so slowly, the movie is **interminable**. I **estimate** the filmmakers could have cut at least half an hour out of the movie!

Destiny Masters has nothing we haven't seen in plenty of movies already. I **recommend** you spend your hard-earned cash on something more original and entertaining.

Kevin has a strong opinion about *Destiny Masters*, and he uses lots of power words to let people know what he means. Here they are!

---

ambush (AM-bush) (*verb*)—to jump out of hiding and attack someone.

The bully **ambushed** Jerry by jumping out of the bushes and knocking him down.

 FAST-BREAK FACTS:

- **Ambush** can also be a *noun*. An **ambush** is the act of attacking someone in a sneaky, surprising way. Another word for this is **ambuscade**.
- **Ambush** has a strange background. It's from a French word, *busche*, which means "a stick of firewood." Maybe in the old days, people were **ambushed** by being hit over the head with a stick!

 YOU COULD ALSO SAY:
assault, entrap, surprise

---

cumbersome (KUM-bur-suhm) (*adjective*)—awkward, heavy, or bulky.

I can't move that box of books because it is too **cumbersome**.

 FAST-BREAK FACTS:

- The word **cumbersome** has been around since 1535.
- **Cumbersome** may have come from an old French word, *combrer*, which means "to prevent." Today, **cumber** is a *verb* that means to hinder by being in the way.

 YOU COULD ALSO SAY:
clumsy, unwieldy, ponderous

---

estimate (ESS-tuh-mate) (*verb*)—to guess or give an opinion.

I **estimate** it will take me two hours to finish this project.

FAST-BREAK FACTS:

- This word can also be used as a *noun*. An **estimate** is a guess about how much something will cost, how big it is, or how long it will take. If you use this word as a *noun*, it is pronounced ESS-tuh-muht.
- **Estimate** comes from the Latin word *aestimare*, which means "to value."

YOU COULD ALSO SAY:
appraise, evaluate, assess, reckon

---

interminable (in-TERM-nuh-buhl) (*adjective*)—something endless—or at least it seems that way!

English class was so boring today, it seemed **interminable**.

FAST-BREAK FACTS:

- This word comes from the Latin *interminabilis*. In Latin, *in* means "not" and *terminare* means "to terminate" or "to end." So *interminabilis* means "without end."

YOU COULD ALSO SAY:
ceaseless, unending, continual

loquacious (loh-KWAY-shus) (*adjective*)—given to excessive talk; wordy.

My teacher is very **loquacious** when she explains things.

 ## FAST-BREAK FACTS:

- This word is another contribution from Latin. It comes from *loqui*, which means "to speak."
- The *noun* form of this word is **loquaciousness** or **loquacity**.

 ## YOU COULD ALSO SAY:
garrulous, talkative, verbose

mediocre (mee-dee-OH-kur) (*adjective*)—average.

Carl tries hard on the court, but his play is only **mediocre**.

FAST-BREAK FACTS:

- The *noun* form of **mediocre** is **mediocrity**.
- **Mediocre** comes from the Latin word *medius*, which means "middle."

YOU COULD ALSO SAY:
ordinary, standard

---

rabid (RAH-bid) (*adjective*)—extremely violent or wild.

The team's **rabid** fans swarmed onto the court to protest the bad call.

FAST-BREAK FACTS:

- **Rabid** comes from the Latin word *rabidus*, which means "mad." Not "angry" mad—"crazy" mad!
- **Rabid** can also be used to describe someone who has the disease **rabies**. A person or animal with **rabies** foams at the mouth and acts very strange.

YOU COULD ALSO SAY:
berserk, deranged, fanatical

---

recommend (reh-kuh-MEND) (*verb*)—to suggest or advise.

Dad's friend **recommended** him for the job.

FAST-BREAK FACTS:

- If you **recommend** someone, you've given him or her a **recommendation**. That's the *noun* form of **recommend**.

- The original meaning of **recommend** was "to praise." It comes from the Latin *recommendare*, which means "to commend."

YOU COULD ALSO SAY:
advocate, endorse

---

rugged (RUH-gid) (*adjective*)—rough, tough, and strong.

You have to be **rugged** to climb those mountains.

FAST-BREAK FACTS:

- **Rugged** can also mean uneven or jagged. It comes from an old English word, *rug*. **Rugged** used to mean "shaggy" or "hairy."

YOU COULD ALSO SAY:
craggy, robust

---

scheme (SKEEM) (*noun*)—a sneaky plan.

Kim always has a **scheme** for avoiding her chores.

FAST-BREAK FACTS:

- **Scheme** can also be a *verb*. To **scheme** means to plot something, or to be up to no good.
- Someone who **schemes** could be called a **schemer**. That's a *noun*.
- **Scheme** comes from the word *schema*, which means "arrangement" in both Latin and Greek.

YOU COULD ALSO SAY:
method, strategy, procedure

sullen (SUH-luhn) (*adjective*)—acting gloomy and grumpy.

Sandy was **sullen** after the coach scolded her.

 ## FAST-BREAK FACTS:

- **Sullen** comes from an old English word, *solain*, which means "solitary." *Solain* comes from the Latin *solus*, which means "alone."

 ## YOU COULD ALSO SAY:
brooding, morose, sulky, petulant

---

swagger (SWAH-gur) (*verb*)—to act stuck-up and conceited. **Swagger** often refers to a proud way of moving or walking.

Andy **swaggered** down the hall, acting like a big shot.

 ## FAST-BREAK FACTS:

- Although it's not a common word, a **swaggerer** is someone who—you guessed it!—**swaggers**. This word is a *noun*.

 ## YOU COULD ALSO SAY:
strut, "walk the walk and talk the talk"

Furtive

4

Dear Diary

Joey stole his sister Kathy's diary. Unfortunately, he's having trouble understanding all the power words Kathy used. Here's a sample entry.

Dear Diary,

You'll never believe what happened during lunch today. I was eating my sandwich when I noticed Nathan sneaking **covert** glances at me from the next table. I've never paid much attention to him because he's so **diminutive**. But now he was acting so **furtive**, I wondered what was going on!

Suddenly, he came over and sat next to me. "Hi, Kathy," he said. He was acting really **bashful**. "I **beseech** you to go to the Fall Dance with me."

I was so stunned, all I could do was **gape** at him. I had no **inkling** he liked me this much! My first thought was to say no to this **zany** idea. But then I realized this was no **trivial** matter to Nathan.

"Sure," I heard myself saying. "I'll go."

Nathan's face was **transformed** by a **vibrant** smile. You know, Diary, he's actually kind of cute. Maybe his lack of height isn't so important after all!

Kathy used big words on purpose, just in case her diary ever fell into enemy hands. (And by the enemy, she meant her brother, Joey!) Here's some information about her power words.

---

bashful (BASH-fuhl) (*adjective*)—shy.

Your baby sister is very **bashful** around strangers.

 FAST-BREAK FACTS:

- **Bashful** is from a very old word, *bash*. *Bash* meant "to be abashed" or "to be embarrassed."
- **Bashfulness** is the *noun* form of this word. **Bashfully** is the *adverb*.

 YOU COULD ALSO SAY:
timid, reticent

---

beseech (bih-SEECH) (*verb*)—to beg.

Leah **beseeched** her teacher to give her more time to finish her report.

 FAST-BREAK FACTS:

- This word is from the old English *besechen*, which means "to seek."
- There are two past-tense forms of **beseech**. **Beseeched** is the more common one, but you could also say **besought**.

 YOU COULD ALSO SAY:
entreat, implore, plead

---

covert (KOH-vurt) (*adjective*)—hidden, not done openly.

Spies often use **covert** methods to get information.

FAST-BREAK FACTS:

- **Covert** comes from the French word *covrir*, which means "to cover."
- If you do something in a **covert** way, you are acting **covertly**. **Covertly** is an *adverb*.

YOU COULD ALSO SAY:

clandestine, surreptitious, secret

---

diminutive (duh-MIH-nyuh-tiv) (*adjective*)—teeny-tiny.

Sam looks much too **diminutive** to play basketball.

FAST-BREAK FACTS:

- **Diminutive** comes from the Latin *diminutivum*.
- This word dates from the 1300s—so it's more than 700 years old!
- The *noun* **diminutive** means a shortened form of a name, or a nickname. For example, Nick is a **diminutive** of Nicholas.

YOU COULD ALSO SAY:

miniature, small, minute

---

furtive (FUR-tiv) (*adjective*)—sly, sneaky.

I don't like the **furtive** way those girls are acting.

FAST-BREAK FACTS:

- This word comes from two sources. There's a Latin word, *furtum*, which means "theft," and a Greek word, *phor*, which means "thief." Either way, you get the idea of what **furtive** means!

YOU COULD ALSO SAY:

stealthy, crafty, shifty

gape (GAPE) (*verb*)—to open widely.

Mona **gaped** when we yelled "Surprise!"

FAST-BREAK FACTS:

· The word **gape** comes from the Old Norse *gapa*, which might have come from the Latin word *hiare*. *Hiare* means "to yawn."

YOU COULD ALSO SAY:

gawk

---

inkling (ING-kling) (*noun*)—a hint or a vague idea.

I have an **inkling** we will have a pop quiz today.

FAST-BREAK FACTS:

· **Inkling** comes from a Middle English word, *yngkiling*, which meant "to whisper." There's also an Old English word, *inca*. That means "suspicion"—which is another way to say "hint"!

YOU COULD ALSO SAY:

clue, suspicion, notion

---

transform (transs-FORM) (*verb*)—to change completely.

After he grew six inches over the summer, Monte **transformed** himself into a great basketball player.

FAST-BREAK FACTS:

- This word comes from the Latin *transformare*, which means "to form."
- Here are some more power words you can use to **transform** your vocabulary—**transformable** and **transformative** are *adjectives* that describe something that can be **transformed**. Something that **transforms** is a **transformer** (a *noun*). And when something **transforms**, a **transformation** occurs. That's another *noun*.

YOU COULD ALSO SAY:

alter, change, convert

---

trivial (TRIH-vee-uhl) (*adjective*)—not important.

Stop bugging me with so many **trivial** stories about your vacation!

FAST-BREAK FACTS:

- **Trivial** comes from the Latin *trivialis*, which means "found everywhere."
- You'll often hear unimportant facts called **trivia**. That's a *noun*. Another *noun* is **trivialist**—someone who enjoys **trivia**!

YOU COULD ALSO SAY:

insignificant, inconsequential, petty, picayune

---

vibrant (VYE-bruhnt) (*adjective*)—very bright.

Hannah's bright red shirt is much too **vibrant**!

 FAST-BREAK FACTS:

- The word **vibrant** has been around since 1616.
- **Vibrant** can also mean something is **vibrating**. That's what your eyes feel like they're doing when you look at something **vibrant**!

 YOU COULD ALSO SAY:
brilliant, colorful, intense, vivid

---

zany (ZAY-nee) (*adjective*)—funny in a crazy way.

Ben's **zany** antics made me laugh.

 FAST-BREAK FACTS:

- **Zany** comes from the Italian *zanni*, or clown. *Zanni* is a form of Giovanni, which is the Italian name for John.
- If you act in a **zany** way, you're behaving **zanily**. That's an *adverb*. And the *noun* form of this word is **zaniness**.

 YOU COULD ALSO SAY:
absurd, silly, hilarious

5

Captain, My Captain

Kareem has to write an essay explaining why he should be chosen as captain of the basketball team. Here's what he put together.

I think I have the right **disposition** to be captain of the team. A captain has many responsibilities. One of the most important is to **enforce** the coach's rules. I wouldn't **tolerate** people who didn't follow those rules. **Reprimanding** players who didn't follow regulations would not be a problem for me.

At the same time, I would never show **contempt** or **taunt** a player who wasn't doing his best. And I certainly wouldn't try to **usurp** the coach's power! I would **execute** my job in a respectful and professional manner.

I also have an **avid** love for the game. Sometimes, practicing drills can turn into **drudgery**. It's also easy to let **fatigue** affect your playing skills. I wouldn't be afraid to let my enthusiasm for basketball show, and that would help everyone feel excited and eager to perform his best.

The coach liked Kareem's attitude and chose him to be captain of the team. See what using your power words can do for you?

....

avid (AH-vid) (*adjective*)—really, really eager. We're talking way beyond average here!

Lisa is an **avid** basketball fan who never misses a game.

 FAST-BREAK FACTS:

· This word comes from the Latin *avidus*, which means "to desire" or "to crave."
· The act of being **avid** is called **avidity. Avidity** is a *noun*.

 YOU COULD ALSO SAY:
ardent, zealous, eager

....

contempt (kuhn-TEMPT) (*noun*)—lack of respect.

I have nothing but **contempt** for people who cheat.

 FAST-BREAK FACTS:

· If you feel **contempt** toward someone or something, you are **contemptuous**. That's an *adjective*.
· Here's another *adjective* for you. **Contemptible** is what you call something that you feel **contempt** toward.
· **Contempt** comes from the Latin word *contemnere*, which means "to despise." That's a fancy way to say you hate something.

 YOU COULD ALSO SAY:
derision, disdain, scorn

....

disposition (diss-puh-ZIH-shuhn) (*noun*)—a person's attitude or personality.

Your boyfriend has a nice **disposition** and is fun to hang with.

 ## FAST-BREAK FACTS:

- The word **disposition** dates from the fourteenth century. It's from the Latin *disponere*.

 ## YOU COULD ALSO SAY:
nature, temperament

---

drudgery (DRUHJ-ree) (*noun*)—hard, boring work. Stuff that isn't any fun!

Cleaning my room is the worst **drudgery** I can think of.

 ## FAST-BREAK FACTS:

- A **drudge** is someone who does hard, boring work. **Drudge** is a *noun*.
- **Drudgery** comes from an old English word, *druggen*, which means "to do hard, boring work."

 ## YOU COULD ALSO SAY:
toil

enforce (en-FORSS) (*verb*)—to make sure a law or rule is obeyed.

A police officer's job is to **enforce** the law.

 FAST-BREAK FACTS:

- Here are two *nouns* for you. **Enforcement** is the act of **enforcing**. And someone who **enforces** is an **enforcer**.
- **Enforce** comes from an old French word, *enforcier*. That means "to do something by force."

 YOU COULD ALSO SAY:
administer, implement, demand

---

execute (EK-sih-kyoot) (*verb*)—to put a plan into action.

Tina was happy to **execute** her sister's plan to stay up late.

 FAST-BREAK FACTS:

- This word comes from the French *executer*.
- **Execute** can also mean "to kill someone," especially if the killing is done to follow a legal decision. The process of **executing** a person or a plan is a *noun*, **execution**.

 YOU COULD ALSO SAY:
perform, enact, render

---

fatigue (fuh-TEEG) (*noun*)—extreme tiredness.

After practicing his moves for two hours, Caleb was fighting **fatigue**.

 FAST-BREAK FACTS:

- **Fatigue** can also be used as a *verb*. To **fatigue** someone means to make him or her tired.

- **Fatigue** sounds French, and it is! It comes from the French word *fatiguer*, which means "to fatigue." But the French word originally came from a Latin word, *fatigare*. It always seems to come back to Latin in the end, doesn't it?

YOU COULD ALSO SAY:

exhaustion, lassitude

reprimand (REH-pruh-mand) (*verb*)—to criticize harshly.

The teacher **reprimanded** Tom for not handing in his homework.

FAST-BREAK FACTS:

- **Reprimand** can also be used as a *noun*. A **reprimand** is a scolding.
- This word comes from the Latin *reprimere*, which means "to check."

YOU COULD ALSO SAY:

reprove, chide, rebuke, scold

taunt (TAWNT) (*verb*)—to tease someone in a mean way.

Roger was upset when the boys **taunted** him about his weight.

FAST-BREAK FACTS:

- **Taunt** can also be a *noun*. A **taunt** is an insult or nasty statement.
- **Taunt** comes from an old French word, *tenter*. *Tenter* means "to tempt."

YOU COULD ALSO SAY:
insult, scorn, mock

---

tolerate (TAH-luh-rate) (*verb*)—to put up with something.

My dad can't **tolerate** it when I'm late for dinner.

FAST-BREAK FACTS:

- This word comes from the Latin *tolerare*. *Tolerare* means "to endure."
- The act of **tolerating** something is a *noun*, **toleration**.
- If someone can't **tolerate** things, he or she can be described with the *adjective* **intolerant**.

YOU COULD ALSO SAY:
allow, accept, condone, permit

usurp (yoo-SERP) (*verb*)—to take power by force.

The rebels **usurped** the throne from the king.

FAST-BREAK FACTS:

- This word comes from the Latin *usurpare*, which means "to seize."
- The act of **usurping** is called **usurpation**. And someone who **usurps** is a **usurper**. Both words are *nouns*.

YOU COULD ALSO SAY:
commandeer, supplant

Voracious

6

Pizza Party!

Joelle's class is planning a pizza party for a fund-raiser. Take a look at the news release Joelle wrote to spread the word about the event.

On Friday night, Crestwood Junior High will be having a **contemporary** social event for the whole community. Join us for a fun evening of pizza and entertainment at the school.

Our class has set a **lofty** goal of raising several thousand dollars for a trip. It is **vital** that we raise the money as soon as possible. We **yearn** to take this trip and hope that the **abundant** help of our community will assist us.

We promise to **enhance** your evening by providing **jubilant** entertainment. There will also be a **plethora** of delicious pizza for you to **devour**. So don't be **solitary**! Join your neighbors and bring **voracious** appetites to this **superb** event!

With all those power words, Joelle is sure to convince everyone to come to the party. Let's check out her word jam.

---

abundant (uh-BUN-duhnt) (*adjective*)—occurring in large amounts.

Kobe Bryant has **abundant** talent as a basketball player.

 FAST-BREAK FACTS:

- **Abundant** comes from the Latin word *abundare*, which means "to abound," or be present in large numbers.
- The *noun* form of **abundant** is **abundance**.

 YOU COULD ALSO SAY:
bounteous, plentiful, lavish, ample

---

contemporary (kuhn-TEM-puh-rer-ee) (*adjective*)—modern or up-to-date.

I like **contemporary** music, not old-fashioned tunes.

 FAST-BREAK FACTS:

- Someone who is the same age as you can be called your **contemporary**. Used in this way, the word **contemporary** is a *noun*.
- **Contemporary** comes from the Latin *tempus*, which means "time."
- If you bring something up-to-date, you have **contemporized** it. Since it describes an action, **contemporize** is a *verb*.

 YOU COULD ALSO SAY:
current, newfangled

---

devour (dih-VOWER) (*verb*)—to eat something really fast.

Mike **devoured** his lunch in record time.

FAST-BREAK FACTS:

- English has borrowed a lot of words from other languages. **Devour** comes from the French word *devourer* and the Latin word *devorare*. Both of these words mean—you guessed it—"**devour**."

YOU COULD ALSO SAY:
gobble, gorge, gulp

---

enhance (in-HANSS) (*verb*)—to make something better.

Taking lessons **enhanced** her ability to swim.

FAST-BREAK FACTS:

- This word can be traced back through a lot of different origins. It probably comes from an old English word, *enhauncen*, which came from the Old French *enhaucier*, which might have come from the Latin *inaltiare*, which came from another Latin word, *altus*, which means "high." Whew! That's a lot of history for one word!
- Something that **enhances** can be called by the *noun* **enhancer**. Another *noun* is **enhancement**. You've probably guessed that means the act of **enhancing**.

YOU COULD ALSO SAY:
amplify, intensify, improve

jubilant (JOO-buh-luhnt) (*adjective*)—very, very happy.

Josh was **jubilant** when his team won the championship.

 FAST-BREAK FACTS:

- The *noun* form of **jubilant** is **jubilation**. You could also use another *noun*, **jubilance**.
- **Jubilant** comes from the Latin word *jubilare*. It's similar to an old German word, *ju*, which means "joy," and the Greek *iyge*, which means "shout."

 YOU COULD ALSO SAY:
exultant, ecstatic, joyful, delighted

---

lofty (LAWF-tee) (*adjective*)—very high.

The Empire State Building is a **lofty** skyscraper.

 FAST-BREAK FACTS:

- **Lofty** comes from an Old German word, *luft*, which means "air."
- The *noun* form of **lofty** is **loftiness**.

YOU COULD ALSO SAY:
elevated, noble

---

plethora (PLEH-thuh-ruh) (*noun*)—a huge amount.

We received a **plethora** of prizes for our fund-raiser.

FAST-BREAK FACTS:

- **Plethora** comes from the Greek *plethora*, which means "fullness."
- You'll probably never hear this word in everyday speech, but the *adjective* form of **plethora** is **plethoric**.

YOU COULD ALSO SAY:
abundance, profusion, plenty, glut, surfeit

---

solitary (SAH-luh-ter-ee) (*adjective*)—all alone.

Katie is pretty **solitary**; she's rarely part of a crowd.

FAST-BREAK FACTS:

- **Solitary** is another English word that originally came from Latin. In Latin, the word *solus* means "alone."
- Have you ever heard of card games called **solitaire**? That *noun* is a name for games that can be played by one person.
- Here's another **solitary** *noun*—**solitude** is the act of being alone.

YOU COULD ALSO SAY:
lone, aloof, isolated

---

superb (soo-PURB) (*adjective*)—incredibly, wonderfully, totally great.

Leroy played a **superb** game last night and helped his team win.

 ## FAST-BREAK FACTS:

- If you do something in a **superb** way, you've done it **superbly**. **Superbly** is an *adverb*.
- This word comes from the Latin *superbus*, which means "excellent." *Superbus*, in turn, comes from joining the Latin words *super* (meaning "above") and *bus* (meaning "to be").

 ## YOU COULD ALSO SAY:
excellent, marvelous, splendid, admirable, magnificent

---

vital (VYE-tuhl) (*adjective*)—very important.

It's **vital** that you attend this meeting if you want to be on the team.

 ## FAST-BREAK FACTS:

- **Vital** comes from the Latin *vitus*, which means "life."
- If someone is lively, you can say he or she has a lot of **vitality**. That word is a *noun*.
- **Vital** signs are the signs of life, such as breathing and heartbeat. These things are important, or **vital**, to staying alive.

 ## YOU COULD ALSO SAY:
critical, indispensable, essential, fundamental

---

voracious (voh-RAY-shuss) (*adjective*)—having a huge appetite.

Conor is so **voracious**, he ate a whole apple pie!

 ## FAST-BREAK FACTS:

- This word comes from the Latin *vorare*. *Vorare* means "to devour."
- If someone is **voracious**, you could say he or she has a lot of **voracity**. **Voracity** is a *noun*. An *adverb*, **voraciously** describes the act of doing something in a **voracious** way.

 ## YOU COULD ALSO SAY:
ravenous, insatiable, enthusiastic

---

yearn (YURN) (*verb*)—to wish for something very strongly.

Liz **yearned** to see her boyfriend while he was away on vacation.

 ## FAST-BREAK FACTS:

- **Yearning** is a *noun* that means "wanting something very badly."
- **Yearn** comes from a few different sources. One is the Old German *geron*, which means "to desire." There's also a Latin word, *hortari*, which means "to urge" or "to encourage." Finally, the Greek word *chairein* means "to rejoice."

 ## YOU COULD ALSO SAY:
long, crave, desire, want

Indignant

7

I Object!

Rick was very angry about a school rule. So he wrote a letter to the principal to express his feelings.

Dear Mr. Brandt:

My classmates and I are very **indignant** about the rule that says we are not allowed to gather on the school steps. We feel this rule is **archaic** and should be changed.

Because students cannot go into the school building until 8:00, those of us who arrive on early buses have no place to gather before school. We don't want to **lurk** on the city streets. And we **loathe** gathering on the playground with the little kids. Anyway, there is not enough room there. We feel the bigger kids put the younger ones in **peril** when we all try to play together in such a small space. This overcrowding is a **detriment** to all students.

We also feel the **penalty** for sitting on the school steps is **obnoxious**. Students shouldn't have to go to detention just because we took **refuge** on the steps.

I understand that **eventually** we will move to a bigger school. In the **interval**, we are stuck in a small space. Let's **abolish** an out-of-date rule that doesn't apply anymore. The result will be a happier student body!

Sincerely,

Rick Valdez

The school principal couldn't help taking Rick's letter seriously, because he used so many power words! Let's check out what he wrote.

....

abolish (uh-BOH-lish) (*verb*)—to get rid of something, once and for all.

If only teachers would **abolish** homework, I'd be a lot happier.

FAST-BREAK FACTS:

- **Abolish** has a confusing background. It's probably from a Latin word, *abolere*, which is connected to another Latin word that means "to grow up."
- Getting rid of something can be called **abolishment** or **abolition**.

YOU COULD ALSO SAY:
cancel, eradicate

....

archaic (ar-KAY-ik) (*adjective*)—very old-fashioned or out of date.

Those rules seem so **archaic**, I don't know why we have to follow them anymore.

FAST-BREAK FACTS:

- This word comes from the Greek word *archaios*.
- **Archaic** may mean old, but the word itself isn't that old. It was first recognized in 1832. That's pretty recent when you look at word histories!

YOU COULD ALSO SAY:
ancient, obsolete, antiquated

....

detriment (DEH-trih-ment) (*noun*)—something harmful.

Smoking is a **detriment** to your health.

FAST-BREAK FACTS:

- If something is a **detriment**, you can describe it with the *adjective* **detrimental**.
- **Detriment** comes from the Latin *deterere*, which means "to wear away."

YOU COULD ALSO SAY:
drawback, disadvantage, impairment, liability

---

eventually (ih-VEN-shuh-wuhl-ee) (*adverb*)—at long last.

Eventually the long practice was over, and I could go home for dinner.

FAST-BREAK FACTS:

- Something that might happen in the future can be called an **eventuality**. That word is a *noun*.
- The word **eventually** has been around since 1680.
- **Eventually** comes from the Latin word *evenire*, which means "to happen."

YOU COULD ALSO SAY:
consequently, finally, ultimately

---

indignant (in-DIG-nuhnt) (*adjective*)—feeling upset because something is unfair.

Sam was **indignant** that he had to go to bed at the same time as his baby brother.

 ## FAST-BREAK FACTS:

- The *noun* form of **indignant** is **indignation**.
- This word comes from the Latin *indignus*, which means "unworthy."

 ## YOU COULD ALSO SAY:
angry, irate, offended, piqued

---

interval (IN-tur-vuhl) (*noun*)—the time between two events.

Elizabeth did her homework in the **interval** between games.

 ## FAST-BREAK FACTS:

- **Interval** comes from the Latin *intervallum*. An *intervallum* was the space between ramparts, or towers, on a wall.

 ## YOU COULD ALSO SAY:
interim, interlude

---

loathe (LOHTH) (*verb*)—to dislike something an awful lot.

Nina **loathed** getting up early and preferred to sleep in.

 ## FAST-BREAK FACTS:

- The feeling you have when you **loathe** something is called **loathing**. That's a *noun*.
- If something is really horrible, you might describe it with the *adjective* **loathsome**.

- **Loathe** comes from the old English word *lathian*, which means "to dislike."

YOU COULD ALSO SAY:
hate, despise, abhor, detest

---

lurk (LURK) (*verb*)—to hide, especially if you're up to no good.

The thieves **lurked** behind the house until they were sure it was empty.

FAST-BREAK FACTS:

- **Lurk** comes from an old German word, *luren*, which means "to lie in wait."
- Someone who **lurks** can be called a **lurker**. Since it refers to a person, **lurker** is a *noun*.

YOU COULD ALSO SAY:
skulk, prowl, sneak

---

obnoxious (ahb-NOK-shuhss) (*adjective*)—very annoying or disgusting.

My little brother is so **obnoxious** when he snoops in my room!

FAST-BREAK FACTS:

- **Obnoxious** comes from two Latin words put together: *ob*, meaning "in the way of," and *noxa*, meaning "harm." *Noxa* also gives us the word **noxious**, which means "harmful" or "poisonous."
- The word **obnoxious** has been around since 1597.

YOU COULD ALSO SAY:
objectionable, offensive, revolting

---

penalty (PEH-nuhl-tee) (*noun*)—punishment.

Charles received a **penalty** for shoving another player.

 FAST-BREAK FACTS:

- **Penalty** comes from the Latin *poenalis*.
- If you give someone a **penalty**, you **penalize** him or her. **Penalize** is a *verb*.

 YOU COULD ALSO SAY:
disciplinary action

---

peril (PEHR-uhl) (*noun*)—danger.

During the storm, our house was in **peril** of being washed away.

 FAST-BREAK FACTS:

- **Peril** comes from a Latin word, *periculum*, which means "fear."
- If you put someone in danger you **imperil** them. **Imperil** is a *verb*. And if something is dangerous, you could describe it with the *adjective* **perilous**.

 **YOU COULD ALSO SAY:**
hazard, jeopardy, threat

refuge (REH-fyooj) (*noun*)—protection or shelter.

We took **refuge** on the deck when it began to rain.

 ## FAST-BREAK FACTS:

- This word comes from the Latin *refugere*, which means "to escape."
- Someone who leaves home to escape war or another severe danger is called a **refugee**.

 ## YOU COULD ALSO SAY:
haven, sanctuary

8

Big News on the Home Front

Eva is sending a long e-mail to her sister to tell her what's been happening at home. Here's what Eva had to say.

Dear Michelle,

This message is **urgent**, so read it right away! You wouldn't believe what's been going on at home. Dad has been acting really **agitated** and **frantic** lately. Mom said he was just tired, but I was sure that was a **euphemism** for what was really going on.

Then the other night Dad came home acting really **horrid**. I knew something was up, so I **interrogated** him. Finally, he admitted that he had lost his job. He was really worried and didn't know what to do.

But the next day, something **extraordinary** happened. You know how Uncle Bill has been **tormenting** Dad to join his Internet company? Well, Uncle Bill called again and said he had just the right position for Dad. This time, Dad wasn't **reticent** about the job. He talked to Uncle Bill for a long time, and then he accepted the job!

Dad **calculates** that he will make more money at this new job. Best of all, he'll be able to work from home part of the week. So losing his job turned out to be a **boon** for everyone. I think the whole thing is pretty **cosmic**, don't you?

Love,

Eva

Eva sure knows how to use her power words! Here's what all those words meant.

---

agitate (AH-juh-tate) (*verb*)—to make someone nervous and worried.

It **agitates** Mom when we come home late.

 ## FAST-BREAK FACTS:

- **Agitate** comes from the Latin *agere*, which means "to drive."
- If you are **agitated**, you are in a state of **agitation**. **Agitation** is a *noun*.

 ## YOU COULD ALSO SAY:
disturb, excite

---

boon (BOON) (*noun*)—something that makes life easier.

Getting my driver's license was a real **boon**.

 ## FAST-BREAK FACTS:

- **Boon** comes from an Old Norse word, *bon*, which means "petition." There's also an old English word, *ben*, which means "prayer."

 ## YOU COULD ALSO SAY:
advantage, benefit

---

calculate (KAL-kyuh-late) (*verb*)—to work something out using math.

I **calculate** that we will save five dollars a week if we walk to school instead of taking the bus.

 ## FAST-BREAK FACTS:

- **Calculate** comes from a Latin word, *calculus*, which means "pebble." You may be thinking, "What does a pebble have to do with math?" A long time ago, pebbles were used in counting. So you never know where a word can come from!
- If you **calculate** something, you've done a **calculation**. That's a *noun*.

 ## YOU COULD ALSO SAY:
compute, reckon, figure

---

cosmic (KOZ-mik) (*adjective*)—relating to the universe. **Cosmic** can also mean something incredibly wonderful.

Jake thought making the team was a **cosmic** experience.

 ## FAST-BREAK FACTS:

- **Cosmic** comes from the Greek *kosmos*. *Kosmos* means "universe." The English word for "universe" is **cosmos**—same pronunciation, different spelling.

 ## YOU COULD ALSO SAY:
great, awesome

---

euphemism (YOO-fuh-mih-zuhm) (*noun*)—a word or expression that is used in place of another. You use **euphemisms** when you want to say something more nicely, or avoid hurting someone's feelings.

When Mark said he was tired, I knew it was just a **euphemism** for feeling bored.

 ## FAST-BREAK FACTS:

- The word **euphemism** comes from the Greek *euphemos*, which means "sounding good."
- Someone who uses **euphemisms** is a **euphemist**. That word is a *noun*. The act of using **euphemisms** can be described by the *verb* **euphemize**.

 ## YOU COULD ALSO SAY:
synonym

---

extraordinary (ek-STROR-duhn-er-ee) (*adjective*)—really unusual or fantastic.

Ben has an **extraordinary** talent for grabbing rebounds.

 ## FAST-BREAK FACTS:

- The word **extraordinary** sounds pretty much the same in Latin. The Latin word is *extraordinarius*, or "more than ordinary."
- The word **extra** is probably a shortened form of **extraordinary**.
- If you do something in an **extraordinary** way, you are acting **extraordinarily**. That's an *adverb*.

 ## YOU COULD ALSO SAY:
amazing, phenomenal, remarkable, uncommon

frantic (FRAN-tik) (*adjective*)—wildly nervous or afraid.

William was **frantic** when his mom had to go to the hospital.

 ## FAST-BREAK FACTS:

- **Frantic** comes from an old English word, *frenetik*, which means "insane." *Frenetik* also gives us the modern word *frenetic*.
- The *adverb* form of **frantic** is **frantically**. **Frantically** means to do something in a **frantic** way.

 ## YOU COULD ALSO SAY:
hysterical, distraught, frenzied

horrid (HOR-id) (*adjective*)—awful or horrible.

My sister's cooking is unbelievably **horrid**—she burns everything!

FAST-BREAK FACTS:

· **Horrid** and **horrible** come from the same Latin word. That word is *horrere*.

YOU COULD ALSO SAY:
repulsive, loathsome, vile, dreadful

---

interrogate (in-TER-uh-gate) (*verb*)—to ask someone detailed questions.

I wish my father wouldn't **interrogate** me every time I come home late.

FAST-BREAK FACTS:

· This word is from the Latin *interrogare*, which means "to ask."
· Here are a couple of *nouns* for you. Someone who **interrogates** is called an **interrogator**. And the act of **interrogating** is called an **interrogation**.

YOU COULD ALSO SAY:
examine, inquire

---

reticent (REH-tuh-suhnt) (*adjective*)—quiet, not willing to talk.

Samantha is the most shy and **reticent** person I know.

FAST-BREAK FACTS:

- **Reticent** is another word with Latin roots. It comes from the word *reticere*, which means "to keep silent."
- The act of being **reticent** is a *noun*, **reticence**.

YOU COULD ALSO SAY:
reserved, subdued, taciturn

---

torment (tor-MENT) (*verb*)—to upset someone on purpose.

Irene loves to **torment** me by cracking her knuckles.

FAST-BREAK FACTS:

- **Torment** comes from the Latin word *tormentum*, which means "to torture." It's also related to another Latin word, *torquere*, which means "to twist."
- **Torment** can also be a *noun*. In that case, it's pronounced a little differently—TOR-ment.

YOU COULD ALSO SAY:
abuse, torture, harass, irritate

---

urgent (UR-juhnt) (*adjective*)—needing attention right away.

Eddie needs **urgent** help if he is going to pass tomorrow's science test.

FAST-BREAK FACTS:

- **Urgent** is from the Latin *urgere*.
- The word **urgent** dates from the fifteenth century.
- If you do something **urgently** (an *adverb*, by the way), you are acting with **urgency**. **Urgency** is a *noun*.

YOU COULD ALSO SAY:
compelling, pressing

9

Drama Queen

Liz wrote a play about something that happened at school. Here's one of the scenes.

ZOE: Hey, Maria, why are you **moping** around today?

MARIA: Oh, no reason.

ZOE: Come on, Maria, fess up. Don't make me **wheedle** it out of you.

MARIA: Oh, all right. I found out that some kids in my history class cheated on our last test. I'm in **turmoil** over what to do.

ZOE: I'll be **succinct**, Maria. You have to tell the teacher.

MARIA: But what if the kids **perceive** I was the one who told? I'll be **infamous** for the rest of the year!

ZOE: But you always said you **abhor** cheaters. Now's your chance to do something about it.

MARIA: I know, but the other kids will be really **vexed** with me.

ZOE: I know it sounds **mundane**, but you have to do the right thing, Maria.

MARIA: I know. Hey, will you come with me to talk to the teacher? If you're there, I won't **waver**.

ZOE: Sure thing! What are friends for, after all?

In Liz's play, the character of Maria is in a tough situation. But Zoe's power words help her see what she has to do. Here's what those words have to say.

---

abhor (ab-HOR) (*verb*)—to hate something or someone. I mean really hate it!

I **abhor** lima beans so much, I'd rather eat spiders!

 FAST-BREAK FACTS:

- **Abhor** comes from the Latin word *abhorrere*, which means "to shudder."
- If you **abhor** something, you feel **abhorrence**. That's a *noun*. The thing you **abhor** can be described by the *adjective* **abhorrent**.

 YOU COULD ALSO SAY:
despise, loathe

---

infamous (IN-fuh-muhss) (*adjective*)—having a bad rep.

Corey is **infamous** for skipping practices.

 FAST-BREAK FACTS:

- **Infamous** comes from the Latin *infamis*. *Infamis*, in turn, comes from the same root as **famous**: *fama*.
- The *noun* form of **infamous** is **infamy**.

 YOU COULD ALSO SAY:
notorious

mope (MOPE) (*verb*)—to act gloomy.

Patty has been **moping** ever since her boyfriend dumped her.

 FAST-BREAK FACTS:

- **Mope** comes from an obsolete word, *mop,* or *mope,* which meant "fool." So if you're **moping,** some might say you're acting like a fool.
- Someone who **mopes** is a **moper**—a *noun.*

 YOU COULD ALSO SAY:
brood, pout, sulk

....

mundane (muhn-DAYN) (*adjective*)—dull, dull, dull.

Mike's weekend was totally **mundane**—all he did was work.

 FAST-BREAK FACTS:

- **Mundane** comes from *mundus,* a Latin word that means "world." If something is "of this world," that means it's ordinary.

 YOU COULD ALSO SAY:
commonplace, uneventful, dreary, humdrum

....

perceive (pur-SEEV) (*verb*)—to understand.

Brad **perceived** that Larry was angry with him when Larry didn't say hello.

 ## FAST-BREAK FACTS:

· **Perceive** comes from the Latin *percipere*, which means "to take thoroughly."
· The *noun* form of **perceive** is **perception**.

 ## YOU COULD ALSO SAY:
discern, comprehend, deduce

----

succinct (suhk-SINKT) (*adjective*)—short and sweet; not wasting words.

Rob's book report was quite **succinct** and took only two minutes to read.

 ## FAST-BREAK FACTS:

· **Succinct** has a fun background. It's from the Latin word *succingere*, which means "to gird." "To gird" means to tie a rope or belt tightly around your waist. See the connection?

 ## YOU COULD ALSO SAY:
concise, pithy, terse

----

turmoil (TUR-moil) (*noun*)—extreme confusion.

After Coach's startling announcement that he was quitting, the locker room was in **turmoil**.

FAST-BREAK FACTS:

- There's a mystery surrounding **turmoil**. No one knows where this word comes from. It entered the English language around 1526.

YOU COULD ALSO SAY:
agitation, chaos, turbulence, tumult, pandemonium

---

vex (VECKS) (*verb*)—to annoy or irritate.

Lou's bad attitude really **vexes** me.

FAST-BREAK FACTS:

- **Vex** comes from *vexare*, which is a Latin word meaning "to agitate."
- Something that **vexes** you causes **vexation**, which is a *noun*. Or you could describe it using the *adjective* **vexatious**.

YOU COULD ALSO SAY:
exasperate, rankle, irk

---

waver (WAY-vur) (*verb*)—to be uncertain.

Tanya's good opinion of Greg **wavered** after he got into trouble at school.

 FAST-BREAK FACTS:

· Here's a word that doesn't have a Latin origin! **Waver** comes from the Old English *waefre*, which means "restless."

 YOU COULD ALSO SAY:
vacillate, fluctuate, falter

---

wheedle (HWEE-duhl) (*verb*)—to convince someone by using flattery or praise.

Karen didn't want to take care of Marv's iguana, but he **wheedled** her into doing it.

 FAST-BREAK FACTS:

· Here's another mystery word. No one knows where **wheedle** came from. But it's been part of the English language since about 1661.

 YOU COULD ALSO SAY:
blandish, cajole, coax, sweet-talk

Mischievous

10

A Really Bad Day

Luke is writing an essay about something that happened at home. He wants to impress his teacher with his big vocabulary.

My Rotten Day

Yesterday had to be one of the worst days of my life, thanks to my little sister, Sarah. Sarah is **mischievous** and always gets into trouble. She doesn't do it on purpose—things just happen **inadvertently**.

Take yesterday, for example. When I got home from school, my mom had left me an **ominous** note. She wanted me to keep an eye on Sarah until dinner. As soon as I read this, my head began to **ache**. Then I heard a crash from Sarah's bedroom. I ran down the hall to see what had happened.

Sarah had knocked over the lamp on her dresser. She was **crouched** on the floor, picking up the **shattered** pieces. "Don't do that!" I yelled. "You'll cut yourself!" I quickly got the dustpan and **restrained** Sarah from helping me pick up the mess.

When I finished, Sarah was gone. Then I heard a **shrill** scream from outside. I **abruptly** stopped what I was doing and ran out. There was Sarah crying because the dog next door had barked at her. Of course, he was only barking because Sarah had tried to **engage** him in a wrestling match!

After that, Sarah fell in a mud puddle, left a trail of wet footprints through the house, and stuffed herself with cookies. By the time Mom got home, we were both **disheveled** and angry. And I got in trouble for everything! There was some good news, though. Mom has **threatened** to never let me watch Sarah again. Now that's the best news I heard all day!

Luke's teacher loved his power words, and his essay. Here's some background.

....

abruptly (uh-BRUPT-lee) (*adverb*)—suddenly and unexpectedly.

John didn't expect Kendra to stop **abruptly**, and he ran right into her.

 FAST-BREAK FACTS:

• **Abruptly** comes from the Latin word *abrumpere*. *Abrumpere* means "to break off."

 YOU COULD ALSO SAY:
hastily, hurriedly, precipitously

....

ache (AKE) (*verb*)—to suffer a dull pain.

Eddie knew he was hurt when his leg began to **ache**.

 FAST-BREAK FACTS:

• **Ache** comes from an Old English word, *acan*. It's been in our language for more than 900 years.
• **Ache** can also be used as a *noun*.

 YOU COULD ALSO SAY:
throb

....

crouch (KROUCH) (*verb*)—to bend your legs and lower your body.

Lenny **crouched** at the foul line to take his shot.

FAST-BREAK FACTS:

- **Crouch** comes from an old English word from the fourteenth century.

YOU COULD ALSO SAY:
bend, squat, stoop

---

disheveled (dih-SHEV-uhld) (*adjective*)—sloppy.

Charlie's **disheveled** hair looks like it's never seen a comb.

FAST-BREAK FACTS:

- This word once was only used to describe hair. It comes from the old French word *descheveler*, which means "to disarrange the hair." Today, **disheveled** can describe anything messy, such as clothes, or even your room.

YOU COULD ALSO SAY:
messy, untidy, unkempt, rumpled

---

engage (in-GAYJ) (*verb*)—to be or make busy doing something.

Luis and Carl were **engaged** in a shouting match when the teacher stepped in to break things up.

FAST-BREAK FACTS:

- **Engage** comes from an old French word, *engagier*.
- The *noun* form of **engage** is **engagement**.

inadvertently (ih-nuhd-VER-tuhnt-lee) (*adverb*)—in an accidental manner.

Hector wasn't looking where he was going and **inadvertently** bumped into Luisa.

FAST-BREAK FACTS:

- **Inadvertently** comes from the Latin word *inadvertentia*.
- When you act **inadvertently**, you do something in an **inadvertent** way—an *adjective*.

YOU COULD ALSO SAY:
rashly, recklessly, negligently

mischievous (MISS-chuh-vuhss) (*adjective*)—playful— but annoying!

The **mischievous** kitten pounced on Tim's shoelaces.

FAST-BREAK FACTS:

- **Mischief** comes from the Old French *meschief*, which means "calamity."
- If you are **mischievous**, you're always getting into **mischief**. **Mischief** is the *noun* form of this word.

YOU COULD ALSO SAY:
impish, naughty, roguish

ominous (AH-muh-nuhss) (*adjective*)—being a sign of bad news; making you feel something bad is about to happen.

Those dark clouds look **ominous**.

 ## FAST-BREAK FACTS:

· The word **ominous** has been around since 1587.

 ## YOU COULD ALSO SAY:
foreboding, menacing, threatening

---

restrain (rih-STRAYN) (*verb*)—to stop someone from doing something.

Leo **restrained** his dog from jumping on the couch.

 ## FAST-BREAK FACTS:

· This word comes from the Latin *restringere*, which means "to restrict" or "to bind tightly."
· The *noun* form of **restrain** is **restraint**.

 ## YOU COULD ALSO SAY:
control, curb, restrict

shattered (SHA-turd) (*adjective*)—broken into tiny pieces.

The glass fell and lay **shattered** on the kitchen floor.

 ## FAST-BREAK FACTS:

• This word dates back to the 1300s. The *verb,* shatter, is from an old English word, *schateren.*

 ## YOU COULD ALSO SAY:
crushed, splintered, smashed

shrill (SHRILL) (*adjective*)—a high, piercing sound.

Martha's **shrill** voice sounds like chalk on a chalkboard!

FAST-BREAK FACTS:

- This word comes from *scrallettan*, an Old English word that means "to resound loudly."
- A **shrill** sound can be called **shrillness**—a *noun*.

YOU COULD ALSO SAY:
penetrating, screeching

---

threaten (THREH-tuhn) (*verb*)—to warn about something dangerous that could happen.

The principal **threatened** to expel my cousin for fighting.

FAST-BREAK FACTS:

- **Threaten** comes from an Old English word, *threat*. And that Old English word comes from the Latin *trudere*, which means "to push." (We always seem to come back to Latin, don't we?)
- If you **threaten** someone, you've made a **threat. Threat** is a *noun*.

YOU COULD ALSO SAY:
warn, intimidate

11

What I Really Think

Cheryl is keeping a diary about her basketball team. Here's what she has to say about her teammates.

LaShandra—way too **vague** about playing defense.

Helen—**ubiquitous** on the court—no one can keep up with her!

Chamiqua—**petite,** but the most **intrepid** player on the team.

Joan—**babbles** to herself while she plays, which distracts everyone—including the other team!

Emily—always **fumbles** the ball.

Jenna—has a **tendency** to **strut** and show off.

Halle—has a lot of weird **quirks**, but can always be counted on.

Tisha—**disintegrates** under pressure.

Annie—needs to work on **rudimentary** skills.

Tammy—seems **lackluster** in her play.

As you can see, Cheryl has some very strong opinions about her teammates, and she uses powerful words to express her feelings. Here's what her comments mean.

----

babble (BAH-buhl) (*verb*)—to talk without making any sense.

Charissa **babbled** excitedly to her friends about the party.

FAST-BREAK FACTS:

· This word is onomatopoeic. That means it sounds like what it means. It comes from the old English word *babelen*.

YOU COULD ALSO SAY:
chatter, jabber, prattle

----

disintegrate (dih-SIN-tuh-grayt) (*verb*)—to come apart; to break into tiny pieces.

The glass **disintegrated** when it hit the stone floor.

FAST-BREAK FACTS:

· This word has been part of the language since 1796. That's not very long ago when it comes to word history! It comes from two Latin words: *dis*, which means "apart," and *integrare*, which means "to make whole."
· The *noun* form of **disintegrate** is **disintegration**.

YOU COULD ALSO SAY:
crumble

----

fumble (FUHM-buhl) (*verb*)—to handle something clumsily.

The crowd groaned when Sam **fumbled** the ball and lost control of it.

FAST-BREAK FACTS:

- **Fumble** comes from an old Swedish word, *fumla*. *Fumla* means "to fumble"!
- The word **fumble** can also be used as a *noun*.

YOU COULD ALSO SAY:
blunder, botch, muff, bungle

---

intrepid (in-TREH-pid) (*adjective*)—brave, bold, clever.

The hero of the movie made an **intrepid** escape from prison.

FAST-BREAK FACTS:

- This word comes from two Latin words: *in*, which means "not," and *trepidus*, which means "alarmed." *Trepidus* also gives us the word **trepidation**, which means "worry" or "fear."

YOU COULD ALSO SAY:
dauntless, doughty, valiant

---

lackluster (LAK-luhss-tur) (*adjective*)—without brilliance or vitality.

Neil's performance on the court was **lackluster**, so his coach benched him.

FAST-BREAK FACTS:

- This word has been around since about 1600.
- The word **luster** means "shine." So **lackluster** literally means "lacking shine."

YOU COULD ALSO SAY:
dull, indifferent, mediocre

petite (peh-TEET) (*adjective*)—small and thin.

Your sister is so **petite**, she looks much younger than her age.

 FAST-BREAK FACTS:

· **Petite** is the English form of the French word *petit*. Just as in English, *petit* in French means "small."
· The *noun* form of **petite** is **petiteness**.

 YOU COULD ALSO SAY:
diminutive, miniature, tiny

---

quirk (KWERK) (*noun*)—a strange quality or way of behaving.

My brother has many **quirks** that make him difficult to get along with.

 FAST-BREAK FACTS:

· **Quirk** is another mystery word—no one is sure where it came from or how it entered the English language.
· If someone has a lot of **quirks**, you could describe him or her with the *adjective* **quirky**. The state of being **quirky** is called **quirkiness**. That word is a *noun*.

 YOU COULD ALSO SAY:
idiosyncrasy, peculiarity, foible

---

rudimentary (roo-duh-MEN-tuh-ree) (*adjective*)—basic.

To become a great player, first you have to master **rudimentary** skills.

 FAST-BREAK FACTS:

· This word comes from the Latin *rudimentum*, which means" beginning."

- The *noun* form of **rudimentary** is **rudiment**.

YOU COULD ALSO SAY:
elementary, fundamental, primary

---

strut (STRUHT) (*verb*)—to walk in a proud or conceited way.

After he won the free-throw contest, Jorge **strutted** off the court.

FAST-BREAK FACTS:

- This word comes from the Old English *strutian*, which means "to exert oneself." It's also related to an old German word, *strozzen*, which means "to be swollen."
- Someone who **struts** can be called a **strutter**—a *noun*.

YOU COULD ALSO SAY:
swagger

---

tendency (TEN-duhn-see) (*noun*)—an inclination to a certain behavior.

Brian has a **tendency** to exaggerate his accomplishments whenever he talks about himself.

FAST-BREAK FACTS:

- **Tendency** comes from the Latin *tendere*.

YOU COULD ALSO SAY:
proclivity, penchant, inclination

---

ubiquitous (yoo-BIH-kwuh-tuss) (*adjective*)—being everywhere at once.

The ads for that new brand of sneakers are certainly **ubiquitous**—I see them every time I watch TV.

 ## FAST-BREAK FACTS:

- This word comes from the Latin *ubique*, which means "everywhere."
- The *noun* form of **ubiquitous** is **ubiquitousness**.

 ## YOU COULD ALSO SAY:
pervasive, widespread, omnipresent

---

vague (VAYG) (*adjective*)—not clear.

Dan was **vague** about where he would meet us, so we never hooked up with him.

 ## FAST-BREAK FACTS:

- **Vague** comes from the Latin *vagus*, which means "wandering."
- If you conduct yourself in a **vague** way, then you are acting **vaguely**—an *adverb*

 ## YOU COULD ALSO SAY:
ambiguous, indistinct, obscure, nebulous

12

My Hero

Yousef had to write a short essay about a person he admired. He chose his grandfather. Here's what he had to say.

A **Profile** of My Grandfather

My grandfather may seem like a **benign** and **quaint** old man. Yet behind his **decorum** lies the heart of a **rascal**! Grandpa loves to play tricks on people. His **remedy** for a bad mood is to make someone laugh in whatever way he can. Grandma used to **scold** him for his antics, but she gave up long ago.

Grandpa also has many talents. When we go camping together, he can **kindle** a fire without using matches. He also grows **fragrant** roses in his beautiful garden.

I try to **imitate** my grandfather in every way I can. Like him, I want to leave beauty and laughter in the world. If I can do that, my life will be a **triumph**.

Doesn't Yousef's grandfather sound like a nice guy? Let's look at Yousef's power words to learn more about his grandfather.

benign (bih-NINE) (*adjective*)—of a gentle disposition.

Jack's dog looks mean, but he's really **benign** and friendly.

 ## FAST-BREAK FACTS:

- **Benign** comes from the Latin word *benignus*. The root word of *benignus* is *bene*, which means "good."
- The state of being **benign** can be called **benignity**—a *noun*.

 ## YOU COULD ALSO SAY:
benevolent, kind, favorable, gracious

decorum (dih-KORE-uhm) (*noun*)—good taste or politeness.

My mother insists I always behave with **decorum**, especially when we have company.

FAST-BREAK FACTS:

- **Decorum** comes from the Latin word *decorus*.
- Something that is done with **decorum** is described as decorous (an *adjective.*)

YOU COULD ALSO SAY:
propriety, etiquette

---

fragrant (FRAY-gruhnt) (*adjective*)—smelling sweet.

Lisa's **fragrant** perfume smells wonderful.

FAST-BREAK FACTS:

- This word comes from the Latin word *fragrare*, which means—you guessed it—"to be fragrant."
- The *noun* form of this word is **fragrance. Fragrance** is a fancy word for "perfume."

YOU COULD ALSO SAY:
aromatic, perfumed, redolent, scented

---

imitate (IH-muh-tate) (*verb*)—to copy someone or something.

Carla's little brother looks up to her so much, he **imitates** everything she does.

FAST-BREAK FACTS:

- This word is from the Latin *imitari*, which means "image."
- **Imitation** is the *noun* form of **imitate**.

YOU COULD ALSO SAY:

duplicate, simulate, mimic

---

kindle (KIN-duhl) (*verb*)—to start a fire. We're talking either physically or emotionally.

Ken's interest in science was **kindled** by a visit to the museum.

FAST-BREAK FACTS:

- **Kindle** comes from an Old Norse word, *kynda. Kynda* is similar to an Old German word that means "fire."
- Material used to start a fire is called **kindling**, which is a *noun*.

YOU COULD ALSO SAY:

ignite, spark, arouse, inspire

profile (PROH-file) (*noun*)—a brief description of someone's life.

I read a **profile** of our coach in yesterday's newspaper.

 ## FAST-BREAK FACTS:

- This word comes from the Latin *profilare*, which means "to draw in outline."
- A **profile** is also a side view of a person's face.
- **Profile** can be a *verb* as well. The act of making a **profile** is called **profiling**, another *noun*.

 ### YOU COULD ALSO SAY:
outline, characterization, biography

---

quaint (KWAYNT) (*adjective*)—charming in an old-fashioned way.

We spent our vacation in a **quaint** seaside town, with lots of old houses and antiques stores.

 ## FAST-BREAK FACTS:

- **Quaint** comes from *cognoscere*, which means "to know" in Latin.
- The *noun* form of **quaint** is **quaintness**. If you're looking for an *adverb*, try **quaintly**.

 ### YOU COULD ALSO SAY:
picturesque, enchanting

---

rascal (RASS-kuhl) (*noun*)—a mischievous person.

I never knew Ned was such a **rascal** until I had to baby-sit him all day and he got into all kinds of trouble!

FAST-BREAK FACTS:

· **Rascal** comes from an old English word, *rascaile*, which means "rabble." *Rabble* is an old-fashioned word used to describe peasants or lower-class people.

· Here's another *noun* for you: The act of being a **rascal** is called **rascality**.

YOU COULD ALSO SAY:
imp, prankster, scamp, scoundrel, rogue

---

remedy (REH-muh-dee) (*noun*)—something that makes you feel better.

Valerie said the new headache **remedy** made her feel much better.

FAST-BREAK FACTS:

· This word is from the Latin *remedium*, which means "to heal." Makes sense!

· **Remedy** can also be used as a *verb*. To **remedy** something means to fix it.

YOU COULD ALSO SAY:
cure, medication, treatment

scold (SKOHLD) (*verb*)—to lecture someone in an angry way.

Kelly's teacher **scolded** her for not doing her homework.

FAST-BREAK FACTS:

- **Scold** comes from the Old Norse word *skald*. A *skald* was a poet—someone who had a talent with words and could probably think of some pretty clever ways to yell at people!
- If you **scold** someone, you're giving that person a **scolding.** **Scolding** is a *noun.*

YOU COULD ALSO SAY:
chide, rebuke, reprimand, reproach, berate, upbraid

---

triumph (TRY-uhmf) (*noun*)—a great achievement.

Geting an A in English was quite a **triumph** for Randy.

FAST-BREAK FACTS:

- **Triumph** comes from the Latin word *triumphus.*
- The word **triumph** can also be used as a *verb.* And if you **triumph** at something, you could be described by the *adjective* **triumphant.**

YOU COULD ALSO SAY:
victory, success, mastery, conquest

13

Dear Helpline

Kayla wrote a letter to the Helpline column in her local paper. Here's what it said.

Dear Helpline,

Please don't **grimace** when you hear my problem. It may seem **innocuous** to you, but to me it is very important.

My brother is driving me crazy! To be more **precise**, living with him is **sheer** torture. Every day, he **deposits** his junk in my room. Then I get in trouble for having a messy **realm**. He also **waddles** when he walks and always has some smart-mouthed **retort** for everything I say.

This problem is bugging me so much that every day I **trudge** home in a **lugubrious** mood. If you can help me solve this problem, it would be the **zenith** of my life!

Desperately yours,

Kayla

Wow, Kayla really sounds desperate! I think we need to look at her power words to understand her problem.

---

deposit (dih-PAH-zuht) (*verb*)—to put something down, or put it in a safe place.

Dan **deposited** his money in the bank so he wouldn't lose it.

 FAST-BREAK FACTS:

- **Deposit** is another word with a Latin background. In this case, the Latin word is *depositus*.
- **Deposit** can also be used as a *noun*. And someone who **deposits** is a **depositor** (a *noun*).

 YOU COULD ALSO SAY:
drop, store

grimace (GRIH-muhss) (*verb*)—to show a negative expression on your face.

Ali **grimaced** in pain when he tripped and fell.

FAST-BREAK FACTS:

- **Grimace** comes from an Old English word, *grima*. *Grima* means "mask," which is what your face can look like if you're **grimacing**.
- **Grimace** can also be used as a *noun*.

YOU COULD ALSO SAY:
frown, scowl

---

innocuous (ih-NAH-kyuh-wuhs) (*adjective*)—harmless; not meant to hurt.

Amy's comment seemed **innocuous**, but I knew she meant to hurt my feelings.

FAST-BREAK FACTS:

- This word comes from the Latin *innocere*, which means "not to harm." *Innocere* also gives us the word *innocent*.
- Something that is done in an **innocuous** way is done **innocuously**, which is an *adverb*. And the state of being **innocuous** is **innocuousness**—a *noun*.

YOU COULD ALSO SAY:
innocent, inoffensive

---

lugubrious (loo-GOO-bree-uhs) (*adjective*)—gloomy.

Deena tried to cheer up her sister and get her out of her **lugubrious** mood.

 ## FAST-BREAK FACTS:

- **Lugubrious** comes from *lugere*, the Latin word for "to mourn." It's also similar to a Greek word, *lygros*, which means "mournful."
- Ready for some other forms of this word? Try the *noun* **lugubriousness**, or the *adverb* **lugubriously**.

 ## YOU COULD ALSO SAY:
dismal, melancholy, mournful

---

precise (prih-SYSE) (*adjective*)—exact or accurate.

Please tell me the **precise** time, exactly to the minute.

 ## FAST-BREAK FACTS:

- **Precise** comes from the Latin *praecidere*, which means "to cut off."
- Something that is done **precisely** (an *adverb*) is done with **precision** (a *noun*).

 ## YOU COULD ALSO SAY:
definite, distinct, particular

realm (RELM) (*noun*)—an area of interest or control, or a special world.

The novel takes place in a fantasy **realm** filled with dragons and monsters.

FAST-BREAK FACTS:

- This word comes from the Old French *reialme. Reialme,* in turn, comes from the Latin *regimen*, which means "rule." By the way, there's also an English word *regimen*, which means "a regular plan or routine."

YOU COULD ALSO SAY:
domain, dominion, empire, kingdom

---

retort (rih-TORT) (*noun*)—a quick, sharp answer.

Inez got in trouble for her rude **retorts** to her parents' questions.

FAST-BREAK FACTS:

- This word comes from the Latin *retorquere*, which means "to twist back." So when you make a **retort**, you are "twisting back" your words!
- **Retort** can also be used as a *verb*.

YOU COULD ALSO SAY:
comeback, repartee

---

sheer (SHEER) (*adjective*)—total and complete; very steep.

There was a **sheer** drop from the side of the road down a rocky cliff to the sea below.

 ## FAST-BREAK FACTS:

- This word comes from the old Norse *skaerr*, which means "pure."
- Another meaning of **sheer** is "very thin" or "transparent."

 ## YOU COULD ALSO SAY:
absolute, utter, unqualified

---

trudge (TRUHJ) (*verb*)—to walk slowly.

Lily **trudged** to school in the pouring rain with her heavy backpack on her shoulder.

 ## FAST-BREAK FACTS:

- No one knows where the word **trudge** comes from. It appeared in the English language around 1547.

 ## YOU COULD ALSO SAY:
plod, tramp

---

waddle (WAH-duhl) (*verb*)—to walk with short steps and swinging from side to side.

My cat is so fat, he **waddles** when he walks.

FAST-BREAK FACTS:

- This word is a variation of **wade**. Both words describe the same type of motion.
- Someone who **waddles** could be called a **waddler. Waddler** is a *noun*.

YOU COULD ALSO SAY:
sway

---

zenith (ZEE-nuth) (*noun*)—the highest point.

Winning a gold medal at the Olympics was the **zenith** of Mike's athletic career.

FAST-BREAK FACTS:

- This word has a complicated history. It comes from an old English word, *senith. Senith,* in turn, came from an old French word, *cenith*, which came from the Old Spanish *zenit*, which was a variation of the Arabic *samt. Samt* means "way over one's head."

YOU COULD ALSO SAY:
apex, climax, pinnacle